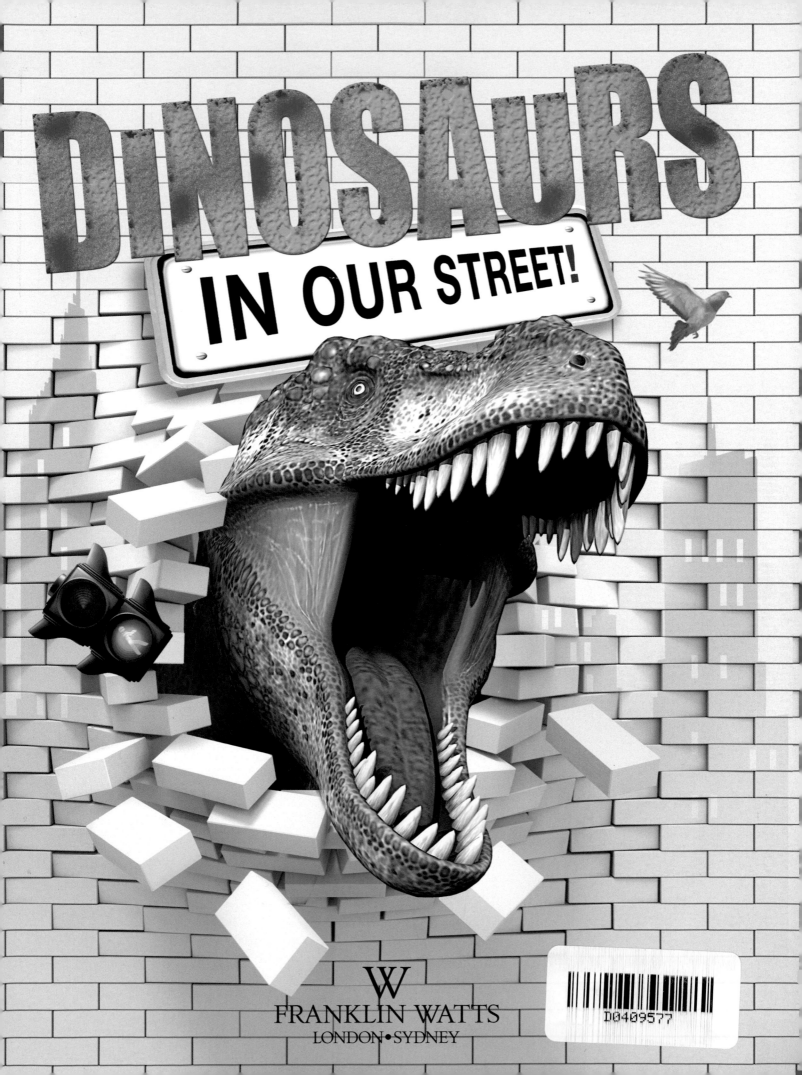

DINOSAURS

IN OUR STREET!

W
FRANKLIN WATTS
LONDON • SYDNEY

Franklin Watts
First published in Great Britain in 2015 by The Watts Publishing Group

Dewey number 523.1

HB ISBN 978 1 4451 4252 4
Library ebook ISBN 978 1 4451 4737 6

Printed in China

DINOSAURS IN OUR STREET!
was produced for Franklin Watts by
David West  Children's Books, 6 Princeton Court, 55 Felsham Road, London SW15 1AZ

Franklin Watts
An imprint of
Hachette Children's Group
Part of The Watts Publishing Group
Carmelite House
50 Victoria Embankment
London EC4Y 0DZ

An Hachette UK Company
www.hachette.co.uk

www.franklinwatts.co.uk

Dinosaurs have come back from extinction and are living in our cities. I know it sounds crazy, right, like something from a movie, but that's exactly what's happened in this book.

Some dinosaurs are small and friendly, but others are fierce and some are huge – so keep your distance – otherwise you might get chomped or stomped on!

Walking down your street will never be the same...

CONTENTS

CARNOTAURUS
say: Kar-noh-TORE-us

With a name that means 'meat-eating bull', this horned dinosaur has a wicked temper. Watch out if you are wearing red! Even red cars aren't safe when this beast is prowling the streets. Just like a bull it will charge at anything that annoys it. It uses its muscular neck and its horns to toss things out of its way.

Don't let those little arms fool you, either. This dinosaur has a set of jaws crammed with sharp teeth. Once it gets hold of its prey, it won't let go!

Period
Early Cretaceous (70 million years ago)

Fossils
Argentina (South America)

Size
7 to 9 metres long; 3.5 metres tall

Weight
1 to 1.5 tonnes

Type
Carnivore

THERIZINOSAURUS
say: THER-ih-zine-oh-SORE-us

Down by the pier a pair of Therizinosaurus are wandering along the shoreline. They use their giant metre-long claws to drag branches from the tall trees.

Although these giants look very fierce they only eat plants – but don't get in their way. If one of them accidentally stepped on you, it would crush the life out of you. It weighs as much as an elephant!

Period
Early Cretaceous (70 to 65 million years ago)

Fossils
Mongolia

Size
5 to 7 metres long; 4 metres tall

Weight
3 tonnes

Type
Probably herbivore

GIGANOTOSAURUS
say: gig-an-OH-toe-SORE-us

When you see this monster coming round the corner of your street, you need to pedal really hard. It is one of the largest carnivores ever to have walked the Earth.

Well-known for its bad eyesight, it smashes everything underfoot with its powerful back legs. These predators usually hunt in packs, which leaves little chance for their prey to escape. Today it is on its own so you're lucky – hurry up and get out of there!

Period
Cretaceous (112 to 95 million years ago)

Fossils
Argentina (South America)

Size
12 to 14 metres long; 5.5 metres tall

Weight
6 to 6.5 tonnes

Type
Carnivore

TRICERATOPS

say: tri-SERRA-tops

Triceratops is the best known of the frilled and horned dinosaurs. Weighing twice as much as a Torosaurus, it needs to eat huge amounts of vegetation to keep its hunger satisfied.

You don't want to get too close to this giant. It is very short-sighted and has a large beak that can break a tree in half. If it thinks it sees a threat, it might charge like a rhinoceros. Those horns have already seen off a few Tyrannosaurus attacks!

Period
Early Cretaceous (65 million years ago)

Fossils
Canada and the United States

Size
8 to 9 metres long; 3 metres tall

Weight
6 to 8 tonnes

Type
Herbivore

TARBOSAURUS

say: TAR-bow-SORE-us

Sometimes you will see this hungry dinosaur going through the rubbish bins. If food is scarce, these meat eaters are great scavengers, eating up the scraps of animals that are already dead.

Tarbosaurus is related to Tyrannosaurus, but does not grow as big. Its vision is not as good, as its eyes do not face forwards like Tyrannosaurus's. But don't let it catch sight of you. It is still a very dangerous hunter!

Period
Early Cretaceous (70 to 65 million years ago)

Fossils
Mongolia and China

Size
10 to 12 metres long; 5 metres tall

Weight
4 to 4.5 tonnes

Type
Carnivore

SUCHOMIMUS
say: sook-oh-mim-us

Take a trip to the park and you might come across this spiky dinosaur wading in the pond. It is looking for its favourite food – fish! Its crocodile-like snout is full of sharp, pointy teeth and it has sharp clawed hands to catch slippery fish.

Don't get too close, though. Just like crocodiles and alligators it would be happy enough to snack on a tasty meat dish, such as a human!

Period
Cretaceous (110 million years ago)

Fossils
Africa

Size
10 to 12 metres long; 4 metres tall

Weight
About 4 tonnes

Type
Carnivore

GIGANTORAPTOR

say: gig-an-toe-RAP-tor

Watch out for this giant feathered hunter. If you come across a pair of Gigantoraptors in the street, make sure you're riding something speedy. They can run very fast when they need to escape predators. Unlike true raptors, they don't have a single larger claw on each foot.

Gigantoraptor eats mainly plants, but don't let that fool you. Its large, grasping clawed hands and powerful beak suggest it also likes an occasional snack of meat.

Period
Late Cretaceous (70 million years ago)

Fossils
Mongolia

Size
8 metres tall; 3.5 metres tall

Weight
1.5 tonnes

Type
Herbivore, occasional carnivore

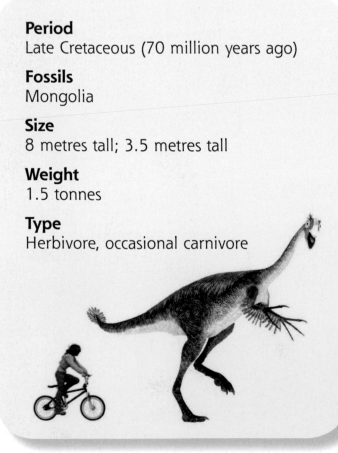

OLOROTITAN

say: oh-low-ro-ti-tan

Olorotitan has a graceful neck like a swan and a colourful crest growing from the back of its head.

People should beware of wearing fashionable hats around this duckbilled dinosaur. When a male's crest is brightly coloured it means he's looking for a mate, so a colourful hat could be mistaken for a rival's crest! No one should make an enemy of this jealous giant!

Period
Early Cretaceous (70 million years ago)

Fossils
Russia

Size
9 to 12 metres long; 4 metres tall

Weight
2.5 tonnes

Type
Herbivore

SAUROLOPHUS

say: SORE-oh-LOAF-us

On a hot summer's day in the city a Saurolophus herd is causing mayhem amongst the traffic. These large, crested duckbills are crossing town on their way to feeding grounds in the park. Like all duckbill dinosaurs they eat plants.

These duckbills have a small crest growing out of the top of their head. They use them to make a unique sound to communicate with the rest of the herd.

Period
Early Cretaceous (70 million years ago)

Fossils
Mongolia and Canada

Size
10 to 12 metres long; 5 metres tall

Weight
2 tonnes

Type
Herbivore

HUAYANGOSAURUS
say: hoy-YANG-oh-SORE-us

A pair of spiky Huayangosaurus have made a nest from rubbish. The female has laid eggs and is waiting for them to hatch. The male patrols nearby to prevent predators from getting too close.

These stegosaurids have spikes at the end of their tails called thagomizers. They can use these like axes, swinging them at predators that dare to approach. So be sure to keep your distance – well away from their tails!

Period
Late Jurassic (170-167 million years ago)

Fossils
China

Size
4 to 5 metres long; 1.5 metres tall

Weight
650 kilogrammes

Type
Herbivore

MICRORAPTOR
say: MIKE-row-rap-tor

Three small dinosaurs glide past a child's window. They have leapt from a tree, scaring away a pair of jackdaws. They use the long feathers on their arms and legs to glide over long distances.

Microraptors' beaks are lined with small teeth. Their favourite food is insects, but they'll eat small lizards and rodents too if they can catch them. Which is great for keeping the pest population down in this part of town!

Period
Late Cretaceous (125 million years ago)

Fossils
China

Size
60 to 85 centimetres; 0.3 metres tall

Weight
1 to 2 kilogrammes

Type
Carnivore

OMEISAURUS
say: oh-mee-sore-us

Some dinosaurs, such as Omeisaurus, have exceptionally long necks. This means they can reach food that other dinosaurs can't, and so get first choice of a fruity snack, five stories high.

Like all sauropods, this dinosaur is ponderous and slow. It doesn't need speed since it is far too big for any predator to attack. Just be careful when you're near this giant though. Its head is so high that it doesn't always see what it's stepping on!

Period
Middle Jurassic (175 million years ago)

Fossils
China

Size
12 to 15 metres long;
9 metres tall

Weight
4 tonnes

Type
Herbivore

PENTACERATOPS
say: pent-ah-ker-ah-tops

Take a trip to the bird gardens and you might come across this amazing beast. Its giant neck frill is brightly coloured to attract a female Pentaceratops, just like a peacock uses its fan of tail feathers.

Pentaceratops has five horns growing from its face: one from its nose, two from its brows and two smaller ones growing from its cheeks. Its frill also has an assortment of spikes and bony nodules arranged along its edges.

Period
Early Cretaceous (75 million years ago)

Fossils
United States

Size
7 metres long; 3.5 metres tall

Weight
4.5 tonnes

Type
Herbivore

COELOPHYSIS
say: seel-OH-fie-sis

A group of speedy Coelophysis chase after fleeing rats. These agile dinosaurs are expert hunters. They have jaws lined with sharp teeth and hands with sharp claws, ideal for grasping small prey. They can move at speed and are very agile, using their long tail to balance as they twist and turn.

But beware! These small predators often form large packs to tackle larger prey. Let's hope the city doesn't run out of rats!

Period
Triassic (230 to 205 million years ago)

Fossils
United States and South Africa

Size
3 metres long; 1.5 metres tall

Weight
50 to 75 kilogrammes

Type
Carnivore

KENTROSAURUS
say: ken-TROH-sore-us

Kentrosaurus belong to the stegosaurid family of dinosaurs. The plates on their backs become long spikes the farther towards the tail they grow. The tail has two very long spikes growing out from the tip that makes it a dangerous weapon.

Keep clear as they cross the road. They even have a pair of spikes growing out from their shoulders. Get too close in a vehicle and the paintwork could suffer.

Period
Early Jurassic (150 million years ago)

Fossils
Africa

Size
3 to 5 metres long; 2 metres tall

Weight
2 tonnes

Type
Herbivore

CRYOLOPHOSAURUS

say: cry-o-loaf-oh-sore-us

Cryolophosaurus is a large meat-eating predator. If you see one of these, run! Although today is so hot it might feel too tired to chase you.

It was formerly nicknamed 'Elvisaurus', after the rock and roll star Elvis Presley. He had a quiff-like hairstyle, like the Cryolophosaurus' crest.

These predators stick to the shady side of the street. They come from Antarctica, where even in Jurassic times the weather would have been cooler.

Period
Late Jurassic (185 million years ago)

Fossils
Antarctica

Size
6.5 metres long; 3 metres tall

Weight
500 kilogrammes

Type
Carnivore

34

DELTADROMEUS
say: del-tah-drohm-ee-us

Down at the beach things can get lively. This speedy predator often hides in the shadows of the pier. When a pterosaur lands on the sand nearby, it rushes out to catch it. It has long slender legs for fast running and a long tail for balance. It has agile arms with grasping hands and jaws lined with sharp teeth, ideal for capturing flying prey in mid-air.

Keep hidden from this dinosaur. It doesn't just eat pterosaurs. In fact, it will eat anything that moves!

Period
Cretaceous (95 million years ago)

Fossils
Africa

Size
8 to 10 metres long; 2.5 metres tall

Weight
2.5 to 3 tonnes

Type
Carnivore

TYRANNOSAURUS

say: tie-RAN-oh-sore-us

These massive predators have jaws crammed with teeth that are 15 centimetres long. They can slice through flesh and crush bones with ease. Their arms are small with two-fingered hands that are useless.

You might catch a rare glimpse of this famous dinosaur in the early morning. At a street crossing a mother keeps a close eye on her juveniles who are just beginning to learn how to hunt. Watch out for that balloon!

Period
Early Cretaceous (75 to 65 million years ago)

Fossils
Canada and the United States

Size
9 to 12 metres long; 5.5 metres tall

Weight
5 to 7 tonnes

Type
Carnivore

OVIRAPTOR
say: OH-vee-RAP-tor

In a back street a female Oviraptor has made a nest to lay her eggs. The male Oviraptor patrols nearby to keep them safe. Be careful! It has sharp claws and its strange beak can give a powerful bite.

When scientists found fossils of an Oviraptor with eggs, they thought it had stolen them and named it 'egg thief'. In fact the eggs belonged to the Oviraptor and it was a caring mother. Its name, though, has not been changed.

Period
Late Cretaceous (80 to 70 million years ago)

Fossils
Mongolia and China

Size
1.8 metres long; 1 metre tall

Weight
25 to 35 kilogrammes

Type
Omnivore

DIABLOCERATOPS
say: dee-ab-low-serra-tops

Like many dinosaurs of the ceratopsian group, Diabloceratops live in small family units or sometimes in vast herds. You don't want to get between a parent and its offspring. They are very protective of their young and are ready to chase away any threat, from cyclists to cars.

Their large array of horns and spikes growing from the top of their frill makes a formidable defence that deters even the hungriest predator.

Period
Early Cretaceous (85 million years ago)

Fossils
United States

Size
6 metres long; 3 metres tall

Weight
About 4 tonnes

Type
Herbivore

BRACHIOSAURUS
say: BRAK-ee-oh-sore-us

Brachiosaurus is a long-necked dinosaur or sauropod whose front legs (arms) are longer than its back legs. It is so big it doesn't have to worry about predators. And it's so heavy you can feel the ground shake as it walks close by.

Brachiosaurus needs to eat more than 182 kilogrammes of food every day, so it spends most of its life eating. Standing on its back legs, it can reach plants high up on the roof gardens of some of the city's tallest apartment blocks.

Period
End Jurassic to Middle Cretaceous
(145 to 100 million years ago)

Fossils
United States, Africa and Portugal

Size
25 to 30 metres long; 12.5 metres tall

Weight
35 to 70 tonnes

Type
Herbivore

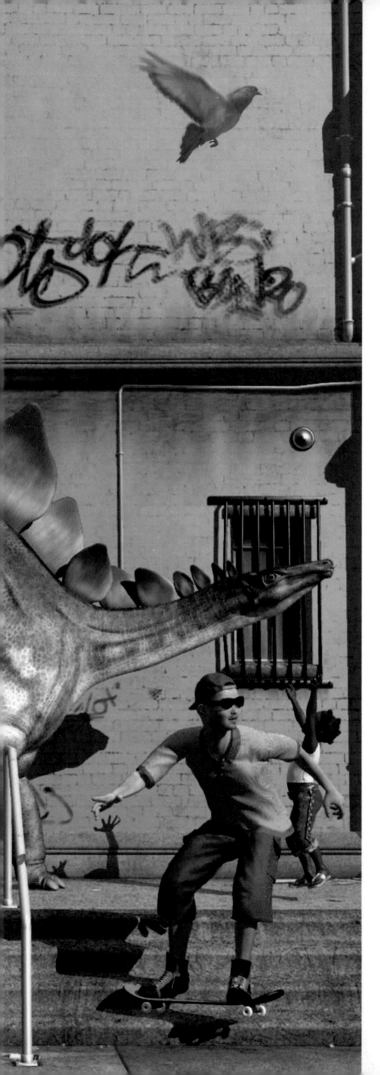

STEGOSAURUS
say: STEG-oh-SORE-us

When fossils of Stegosaurus were first discovered it was thought the plates lay across its back like roof tiles. But actually the petal-shaped plates grow upwards from the skin on its back. They work like a car's radiator. The warm blood running through its plates radiates heat into the colder air, and so keeps it cool.

Make sure you approach this dinosaur from the front. The back end has a nasty thagomizer – a spiked tail.

Period
Early Jurassic (155 to 137 million years ago)

Fossils
United States

Size
7 to 9 metres long; 4 metres tall

Weight
2 to 4 tonnes

Type
Herbivore

POLACANTHUS
say: POH-luh-KAN-thus

A Polacanthus has rows of spikes running down the length of its body, except for a large area on its back, above its hips. Here it has a layer of thick bone which makes a perfect place to sit!

These plant-eating ankylosaurian dinosaurs have very thick, leathery skin and are quite harmless. But be sure to stay away from their powerful tail when they're agitated.

Period
Late Cretaceous (115 million years ago)

Fossils
Europe

Size
4 to 5 metres long; 1.5 metres tall

Weight
900 kilogrammes

Type
Herbivore

ALTIRHINUS
say: al-tih-RYE-nus

This strange-looking dinosaur has a nose that it can blow up like a balloon. It does this to attract female Altirhinus. It is a plant-eating dinosaur that is quite at ease walking on its two back legs or on all fours. It has a spike on each hand instead of a thumb which it uses as a defensive weapon.

Altirhinus has similar feeding habits to cows and horses. Although it has a wide-beaked mouth, it grazes on low-lying plants.

Period
Late Cretaceous (125 to 110 million years ago)

Fossils
Mongolia

Size
7 metres long; 2 metres tall

Weight
4 tonnes

Type
Herbivore

UTAHRAPTOR
say: YOU-tah-WRAP-tor

Running along a road a Utahraptor towers above the people on the pavement. This massive raptor has claws on its feet that are 22 centimetres long. It uses them like a knife to stab its prey. It keeps them off of the ground so the points don't become blunted when it runs.

Like other, smaller raptors it is covered in feathers so is probably warm-blooded. It needs the soft downy feathers to keep it warm.

Period
Early Cretaceous (70 to 65 million years ago)

Fossils
United States

Size
7 metres long; 2 metres tall

Weight
0.5 to 1 tonnes

Type
Carnivore

ARGENTINOSAURUS
say: AR-gent-eeno-SORE-us

In the quieter parts of town you may discover a dinosaur's nest. Although it's huge, Argentinosaurus lays eggs that are only the size of a football. The young fend for themselves as soon as they hatch. They take about 15 years to reach adult size though, so you're safe around the hatchlings for now.

Argentinosaurus use their peg-like teeth to strip leaves from the branches of trees. They don't chew, but swallow the food whole, which gets ground up by stones in their stomach.

Period
Middle Cretaceous (100 million years ago)

Fossils
Argentina

Size
30 to 35 metres long;
7 metres tall

Weight
73 to 83 tonnes

Type
Herbivore

DEINONYCHUS

say: die-NON-i-kuss

Deinonychus has big hands with sharp claws to hold on to its prey. On each foot it has a large sickle-shaped claw to stab its victims. It keeps this claw off the ground when it moves so it doesn't get blunt.

Roaming in packs, these intelligent dinosaurs are terrifying hunters that can bring down animals many times their size. Arrays of long feathers on their tails, arms and heads are used to signal to one another. Do not approach – these animals are deadly.

Period
Late Cretaceous (115 to 105 million years ago)

Fossils
United States

Size
3 metres long; 1.5 metres tall

Weight
60 to 75 kilogrammes

Type
Carnivore

TOROSAURUS
say: tor-oh-SORE-us

A giant among the frilled and horned dinosaurs, Torosaurus is a powerful animal. With its massive horns, it is used to getting its own way, even when its path is blocked.

Its large frill is not all bone as there are two large holes in it. The holes are covered with leathery skin which can blush red when blood is pumped through blood vessels in the frill. Keep clear of this hefty dinosaur when it's in a bad mood.

Period
Early Cretaceous (80 to 70 million years ago)

Fossils
Canada and the United States

Size
7.5 metres long; 2.5 metres tall

Weight
6.5 tonnes

Type
Herbivore

CORYTHOSAURUS

say: koh-rith-OH-sore-us

This duckbill's name means 'helmet lizard' because its crest looks like an ancient Greek helmet. Its crest is full of hollow spaces. It uses it like a fog horn to amplify calls that warn its herd of predators. Like all duckbills, it is a plant eater and spends its life on all fours while feeding among a large herd.

Quick, make a run for it. This one is running on two legs and using its fog horn, which means there's a predator chasing it! Danger!

Period
Early Cretaceous (75 million years ago)

Fossils
Canada and the United States

Size
10 metres long; 4 metres tall

Weight
4 tonnes

Type
Herbivore

DIPLODOCUS

say: DIP-low-DOCK-us

The local emergency services are needed to free this Diplodocus. It has wandered into a back street and tangled its tail in the overhead cables. This is the longest of any dinosaur – and has the longest tail. At around 14 metres, its tail is about half the dinosaur's total length. It uses it as a whip, cracking it in the face of predators to scare them off.

It's lucky the cables aren't electric or it might have got a nasty shock!

Period
End of the Jurassic (150 million years ago)

Fossils
United States

Size
25 to 30 metres long; 8 metres tall

Weight
15 to 25 tonnes

Type
Herbivore

INDEX